Mariposa De Fuego:

A Journey To Empowerment

DAXSON PUBLISHING

Praise for this book:

"Mariposa De Fuego: A Journey to Empowerment is a rollercoaster ride through the reclamation of Altamarino's self-worth & identity in the form of metamorphosis. "

- Crystal Reyes Lozano
Author of : Wild Flower Blooming

In *Mariposa De Fuego: A Journey to Empowerment* Altamirano takes us on a journey from her childhood, to her father's death, her relationships, and basically how she built herself up from grief and trauma. In her debut poetry collection, she chronicles her battles in life, and entangles the reader to experience the struggle and the empowerment all at the same time.

- Erica B. Castro
Author of: The Pain Left Behind: Surviving a Suicide Loss

Aurea's Poems: From simple words a voice emerges--a woman, a young daughter, a mother, but even more so simply a person--poignantly personal. A unique multilingual and multicultural perspective and a most unique feminism. It is impossible to read this poetry without feeling her pain, without compassion, and without a tremendous lift of spirit from its clarity and hopeful tenderness of life.

- Larry Cohen

Mariposa de Fuego
© 2024 Áurea María Altamirano Cuaresma
ISBN: 9798990053137
Library control number: 2024910699
Cover art: Áurea María Altamirano Cuaresma

First Edition, 2024

Printed in the United States of America

Edited by: Erica B. Castro
Cover Design by: Rachel Kiskaddon
Layout Design by: Rachel Kiskaddon

DAXSON
PUBLISHING

Dedication

I dedicate this book to all women and girls who are going through the journey of transformation and self-discovery. I hope this book helps empower them to continue reconstructing themselves and to inspire them to come out of their cocoons, speak up, tell their story, and fly high. This book is for anyone on the path of transformation.

Mariposa De Fuego:
A Journey To Empowerment

Áurea María Altamirano Cuaresma

Embracing my inner child's dreams.

— Áurea María

Contents

Para quién escribo   4
For whom I write   6

Childhood
A los ojos de un Niño   11
In the eyes of a child   13
New Teacher vs. Third Grader   14
My School Bully Died   22
You Left me Here   25
The Death of *Superniña*   28

Father
Dad   32
Fighting The Bad Fight Again   38
Sorry   39
I Was...   43

Society
No! al olvido y la injusticia   48
No! to oblivion and injustice   50
My Own Soap Opera   52
Female Legs Should Live Without Fear   56
One More Newborn Girl   59
What a Latino Woman Is Supposed to Be   62
Sentenced or Not?   64
My Very Own People   66
They Are Looking At You. Are They Only Dishes?   69
The Other Perspective
Part 2 - Coming From ("They Are Looking At You")   70

Relationships
Loving A Vulnerable Sincere Woman   74
Against time   76
The Most Imperfect Of the Two Of Us   79
The Final Battle   82

Most Powerful Resource 84

The Violence Of Your Silence 85

Where Is ... ? 87

It Is Me, 89

I am who I am ... 91

Enjoying the Flaws 93

Love Me Like I Was Gone Already 96

I Have to Let You Go 98

Self

Soy yo, Siendo una Paloma 102

Being a Dove 103

My Fear, My Enemy, And Friend 104

Personal 108

Dear Poem Of Healing 110

Empowerment

Coming Back After The Gray World 114

I Was Born Alone 115

The Mess Of the House 117

Sing and cry 118

Sprouting My Strength My Wings 120

She Is Coming Out to Shout Her Truth 121

Discovering Me 123

She Is Back 125

Me 126

Acknowledgments

I want to thank everyone who has supported me in my long journey of self-discovery. Including the agreement I made with myself to translate my thoughts to paper. It has been extremely difficult, both the shaping of the poems and the mixture of languages of both English and Spanish. The creation of my first book of poetry *Mariposa De Fuego: A Journey to Empowerment* is the culmination of my battle with writing, and at the same time the beginning of acknowledging myself as a writer. It fulfills the promise I made to my inner child that my writing would see light. When she first wrote her first booklet in elementary school, and the seed was planted

I want to acknowledge the Community Literature Initiative Program (CLI) to Ruddy Lopez, my editor, and Rachel my designer. I want to thank Hiram Sims, James Coats, Lisa Montagne, Brandon Allen, and also my CLI classmates who accepted me as part of their community. A special thanks to Erica Castro, my classmate, and accountability partner, who encouraged me to finally finish this project. I needed her push reminding me how hard I had to work to get something so personally precious done. To my father, César, who is looking over me from heaven, and I am sure is proud. My sister Daisy Yasmin and my mother Felipa, who have received me with open arms in my home country when I needed to recharge and rest my mind, body, and soul. My in-law family, who have been kind enough to give me space to write, and who have helped me with the care of my son. It has been difficult, but the outcome has outweighed the struggle. My therapist Nina, who has listened and helped me survive my grief. To my adult Spanish students and now dear friends Larry, Parke, Ana María, Teo y Mark, who have not only read the poems and gave me their sincere and helpful reviews, but also gave me some advice in life. To my son, Amaru, "you gave me the strength to continue. I did this for you. I wanted to show you an example of persistence and resilience. Amaru, dreams do come true."

Preface

The idea for the book started with a letter to my father, but rapidly I realized I was in the middle of shedding all of my childhood trauma, uncovering many neglected, and buried feelings. I had to learn to leave behind my past and tried to survive by just living my daily life. In my young adulthood, I had promised myself to heal the wounds of my past. Writing this book has helped me heal. I had to leave behind many negative aspects of my life that were responsible for the marks of my chronic depression and anxiety.

I witnessed the fragility of life when my father died at only sixty five, partially a victim of Parkinsons and the negligence of the health care system during the COVID pandemic. I barely was starting to see his real face behind his depression. I was able to see the beautiful soul my father had and understand his perspective. I saw in him a beautiful soul that could not flourish in life, and my repressed dreams of a happy family life in the past that made me reconsider my present life. I had to redefine what my goals in life were. I had to look at the following areas of my life: self-esteem, relationships, family, motherhood, and romantic love. I had to rediscover what I wanted in these parts of my life.

Since my father's passing was abrupt and shocking, it exacerbated my neglected and procrastinated need for healing. My emotional pain became a grenade that exploded and nearly killed me. My awakening came some months before the pandemic in response to my last effort to hold my family together. After years of dysfunction, I tried to keep everything together at home, but nothing would prepare me for my father's death. When you lose someone you love, I urge you to look for help such as grief circles, therapy, or help from supportive family and friends.

I suffered tremendous amounts of despair because I was avoiding dealing with the grief of my father's death. The accumulation of both grief and my trauma almost destroyed me. I realized I needed to practice self-care, so I began therapy. Everyone has a story and nobody really knows the life of others. In dealing with all this pain, I longed to read about other women's journeys, so I could relate to them and perhaps take some advice or just feel that I am not alone. I only hope to inspire other women to start and continue their own journey of self-discovery or rediscovery despite the rocky road. I urge them to speak up, use affirmations, as a main tool for self-empowerment. I have fought to overcome my own limitations and have started my own manifesto for life.

With this book, I also embrace the dreams of my inner child and start to work on fulfilling her destiny. This dream created by and for myself. It is based on my values, and using my own voice. My dream is that all young girls could be cared for, nourished, and encouraged more consciously by their caretakers, so they can have a clearer road to travel. I hope there is healing in women's journeys because of this book. I also hope this book serves as inspiration. Healing is never finished, it is a process that we must continue throughout our lifetime. I hope women can find hope and healing with the help of this book. It is not only poetry, it is the summary of my own learning. This book contains the process of transformation in words, as the result of all the years of therapy and reading I did to heal. It has brought me to this point of awareness. I also hope this book serves as an inspiration to young writers and to others who hope to start the second chapter of their lives. This is the beginning of a new life.

Note:

This book was originally written 60% in Spanish and 40% in English. Some poems started in English and included Spanish, while others started in Spanish and were translated to English. I did all the translations myself. The inspiration comes to me in both languages, so I decided to let my poems be themselves in all their bilingual richness. I also hope to inspire more writers, especially women to write bilingual poems, so they can also be free from the weight of their own lives and feel empowered.

Introduction

This book starts with childhood experiences that left marks in me such as my new teacher's initial rejection, and the school bully who bullied me. Also my best friend, and possible love interest passing away. My noxious exposure to junk press, initiated out of curiosity, but then it robbed me of the innocence of my childhood, and revealed to me the beginning of a more overt femicide taking place in my home city, Lima, which seeded self-doubt in my mind as a young woman.

My journey continues with poems dealing with grieving the loss of my father. He passed away right after the second COVID lockdown in Lima, in August of 2020. This chapter expresses my cries for the lost opportunity of connecting with him, and never creating a healthy father-daughter relationship.

Then, comes the chapter on my relationship. It entails issues with my partner, where our insecurities have formed tormentous attachments and disconnection, that grew and took us to the path of separation. As a painful and fruitful consequence of this web of emotional distress in my life, I was forced to analyze my own life. I had to consider my emotional health and social circumstances. I had to look at all the periods of my life from late adulthood to young adulthood, and my childhood to adolescence. These explorations enabled me to understand the influence of the social barriers imposed on me as a woman by society and how deeply they affected me. Understanding and verbalizing my own frustrations have given me the strength to start my healing. Coming to the conclusion I can do both give back to society and also be truthful to myself, my values, and my ideas.

Finally, the last two chapters, *Self* and *Empowerment*, are the most recent part of my process dealing with my inner work towards healing and the improvement of my self-esteem. I decided to confront my fears, to look at my wounds of childhood and early adulthood in order to rise and recover my power, seeing myself as a vindicator of my lineage and the doer of my future.

Mariposa De Fuego:

A Journey To Empowerment

Para quién escribo

Escribo para ellos,
para mujeres, para niñas,
pero también para los niños.
Para mi hijo.

Escribo para mí.

Escribo por mi dolor,
y de mi dolor;
para entenderlo,
para procesarlo,
para transformarlo.

Para que salga de mí
y salga al mundo.
De sus propias heridas,
florece el brillo de mi alma,
que mi dolor y yo llevamos dentro
para iluminar el camino.
de muchos niños,
ojalá.

Como hubiera querido
que alguien lo haga por mí.

Porque sanarnos a nosotros mismos
sanará nuestro niño interior,
y a nuestros hijos.
Trabajar nuestro pasado
nos deja ver con más claridad nuestro presente,
para sanar nuestro futuro.

Escribo para mi curación,
para construir mi propia felicidad
con mis propias manos.
Para mi redención
y mi propia libertad.

Para volar,
como una paloma.

Como una mariposa de fuego,
que se rehace de sus propias cenizas,
de su propio dolor.

For whom I write

I write for them,
for women, for girls,
also for boys.
For my son.

I write for me.

I write because of my pain,
and from my pain;
to understand it,
to process it,
to transform it.

So it pours out of me
and goes out into the world.
From its own wounds,
it flourishes the shine of my soul,
that my pain and I carry inside,
to illuminate the way
of many children,
hopefully.

As I would have wanted
someone to do for me.

Because healing ourselves
will heal our inner child,
and our children.
Working out our past
let us see more clearly our present,
to heal our future.

I write for my healing,
to construct my own happiness
with my own hands.
For my redemption
and own freedom.
To fly,
like a dove.
Like a butterfly of fire,

that is remade from its own ashes,
of her own pain.

"The eyes of a Child/ Los ojos de un niño,"
by Áurea María. Charcoal, 20 x 25 inches, 2016.

Childhood

A los ojos de un Niño

Todo es posible.
El tiempo jugando y soñando
es eterno.
Es todo.

No tiene peso, ni forma.
El tiempo no existe,
es nada.
No tiene final,
es eterno.

No hay prisa por apurar el paso
pero hay apuro por vivir.
Todo al mismo tiempo.

Nos sentimos invencibles.

Ay, esos tiempos.
Después de los golpes del camino,
somos casi hielo,
almas andantes
hijos de la monotonía,
del día a día por sobrevivir.

Mucho después,
cuando la sabiduría nos alcanza
y nos pega la cacheta
con sinsabor a muerte de un ser querido,
u otras fatalidades,
puede hacer que reaccionemos
y despertemos ese niño.
que éramos,
que habíamos olvidado.

Para abarazarlo
Y sacándonos las lágrimas,
decirle soriendo
que ahora nosotras
estamos a cargo.

In the eyes of a child

Everything is possible.
Time playing and dreaming.
it is eternal,
It's everything.
But its soul
only matters.

It has no weight, no form.
Time does not exist,
it's nothing.
But it has no end,
It is eternal.

There is no rush to speed up the pace,
but there is a rush to live.
All at the same time.

We feel invincible.

Oh, those times.
After the bumps on the road,
we are almost ice,
sometimes walking souls
children of monotony,
from day to day to survive.

Much later,
when wisdom reaches us
and slaps us in the face.
with distaste because our loved one died,
or other fatalities,
It may be that we finally react,
and awaken that child.
that we were,
that we have forgotten.

New Teacher vs. Third Grader

At recess time with my friends,
I am the boss of the territory,
I am at the top of my game.
I can travel by space,
like the Super kitties,
Los Supergatos
or
Wonder Woman.
I fly.

I am the creator of my storyline.

> *"Let's plan. Let's do it.*
> *Ready, run without touching the floor,*
> *pass the abyss, save the prisoners,*
> *restore the peace of our city and our world!"*

Directing my crew of fantastic superheroes,
I am just me,
without apology.

I lead, I flow, I am free.

I am the richest of the poorest,
or the strongest girl in school.
It really does not matter,
I triumph!

I have great power in my fingers,
cual varita mágica
and I can also eat books for snacks, with jelly, yum!

The old bell rings,
I can teletransport right to my seat
in a *chasquido*, of course, zzummp!
Excitement, some small nervousness
and a tiny drop of fear is tickling me!
Today, I have a new teacher.

Let's see!

While waiting at my desk,
I still miss my last teacher, Carmencita.
But even though Mom told me Carmencita wanted to stay,
she could not.
She did not get her teaching permit on time.
That is so unfair!

Mom says it is good to give my new teacher a chance.
I listen to my mom, she knows a lot,
so much, that she is almost always right.

Then, here we go, ready to work!

Attentive with my *antenitas de vinil*
like *el Chapulín Colorado.*
Here come the questions:
The use of articles...
I know the answer.
I raise my hand up high.
First attempt to be seen, it fails.
No problem, I say.

Later, another big chance.
How many provinces in the country?...
So easy...*Mano arriba.* No. *Nada,* nope!
Second attempt does not work.
The third one. *Tampoco.*

Well, tomorrow is another day!

===

Certainly, it is an ok Tuesday.
Recess left me already. The day is passing me by.
By now the child in front of me
and the one behind me have already been chosen.
At the last minutes of class my new teacher's eyes are close to my seat!
I see it. Finally, here it comes...and it passes...
Well, I guess not. Today is not the day.

Mom always says patience helps.
I say, well, ok...
But one moment...maybe I am not being clear,
but how?
I am raising my hand the highest I can,
and I am quite tall,
and more with my puffy ponytail.
Yes! He can see me,
...or maybe not?

Not today.

===

Today is the day. I just know it.
Because it is a sunny, beautiful one.
A bird singing on our poinciana tree outside of my house,
has told me.
You know,
that is good luck.
I woke up early and learned my homework well.
Between history, math, calligraphy,
and language, I swim.
Here we go. Arm high up.
Nada, Plop!
One more time, nope!

How come that bird lied ?
Even the ones that don't want to go, are being called twice.
Did I acquire the invisible superpowers
without realizing?
What is going on?

===

We have already reached Friday,
and by now I am not lifting my arm anymore.

Then, somehow, I heard my name.
Calling out like a dream...
I eagerly answer
4x9 is 36 because ...

Next question, next student, he said.
But let me *finishhh*...I said in my head.
I always explained my answer to Carmencita.
Ugh. Yep! I forgot,
you are not her...

I might have surpassed my invisibility,
but it still feels so unfair and...weird.
I do not feel I have won anything.

     Ok, maybe he is in a hurry...or it is that...
     he doesn't like me...Could it be?
     No, come on! No!...
     He is a teacher. My new teacher.

===

I had to do something...
Wait, I am a pro at calligraphy.
Yes, I am sure it will fix it all.
When he meets my super rounded *A's*, elongated *L's*
and stylized *Z's, V's* and *R's*,
he won't resist it. He won't.

I come out of class wearing a renovated bright smile,
and a fancy plan in my mind.

===

At school, it is Monday,
and some heavy air has been *merodeando*
by the hallways all day,
and it stinks so much that we have to open some doors,
sí o sí.

Some children giggle and hide their eyes from something,

I do not know what is going on.
Well...I cannot investigate now. I am too busy.

===

It is Monday already, the day for my calligraphy bomb.
At revision time, I show not one page.
Pretending, I cannot find the pages,
I go through five pages of previous work.
In my mind, I have already conquered.
He will see it, *jjjiii wwwowooju.*
my calligraphy letters, yea!

> My new teacher– Ok, just show me page forty-five,
> please!

Disaster!
Disappointment is written on my eyes,
but my tears should not leave my *párpado.*

I fight, I contain, I suppress, and I retreat to my seat.

> Breathe, girl, breathe! I encourage myself.

Ayyyay, just now, I am followed by these children bugging me
to teach them to draw letters, uggh!
To add up,
another child pretended he had confused his workbook
with my calligraphy workbook
and almost stole my gold.

> Shake it off, shake it off, girl! I keep telling myself.
> Remember, nobody should steal power from *superniña!*
> Not even these tears that are trying to escape,
> not even the teacher...
> No, no, girl! They can not.

A la salida, I tried to get ahead of the clock.
Mom is taking too long to pick me up.
Mom had stopped at the door
to talk to some of other moms.

I did not wait, I ran to her without Mom seeing me.
Whispers?

What is going on? I slow down. I need to know.
I try to get some *hilo de "la conversación."*

I confirmed my broken heart.
That the teacher said what?
About me?
===
On the
next day,
I enter to an egg-shelled world,
each time closer to the mouth of the monster holding the chalk.
.

My world has flipped, I can barely recognize my seat.
All is gray, where did the bright color go?
Now, school is just where I must go,
where I must show I am not too little of a portion,
to show I am good enough to just belong.
I don't even know how much or how anymore.
Just because of my new *malo* teacher.

It is all his fault!

For him, my Carmencita praised me too much!
... "That I did not do much to deserve such high appreciation."

      Sorry, well, I did not realize that, that was bad!
      For starters, I did not know I was that loved.
      She never told me that directly!

      ... that my past teachers loved me.

      I guess it is good news. They never said it.
      I guess I did not expect them to love me so much.
      But why does it hurt that you do not like me?

            You say I am not that great,
             I am not that smart.
            You think I am a fake.

            You say behind my back that you will unmask me.
            You declare me your enemy.
            You basically declare war on me! Why?

What is wrong with you?

Or is something wrong with me?

Is this real?
You hate me?

Maybe what you hate about me is the sunnied color of my skin.
Or my long neck, because I am taller than all those naughty boys
in school you appreciate so much.
I also am almost taller than you.

Or maybe because I am too serious sometimes.
Maybe I am scary to you?
...Me? ... Maybe.
Sometimes I have felt like a lion,
but I am nice.
Why do you hate me?

It is just me! A child!
And all the rest are my superpowers, just that.

Why do you judge me so quickly?
You just arrived here.
You do not know me.
You do not know where I come from,
or my life outside of school.
You do not know the hours
I spend helping my parents.
I push heavy cargo tricycles
at their *ambulante* store on the weekends.
I spend nights doing homework
by candle light.

This place is my second reign.
And even though the door sounds all squeaky
and our only window look so small like a *calabozo* one,
I will defend my castle from you, the *griffo* contendor!

From now on, I always will bring my two swords
the right answer so fast
and my actual student brigadier baton,

palo de policia escolar.

I did not want to use them in this way before,
But it is just too much,
you do not leave me no other choice.

Along with my belt,
my insignia that will blind you,
if you continue being this mean.
I just wanted you to be my teacher!

But now everything comes handy
to make you respect my land.
You are the intruder!
You are supposed to be on my side,
you are supposed to be my teacher,
my friend.

Why do you do this, why?

It is all so confusing.
I only know
I must defend what is mine!

My School Bully Died

I did not like her.
To me, she was the meanest creature,
I was forced into the most absurd fight,
and I am a true pacifist.

She dared to leave this Earth,
in front of my eyes.
Her naughty *tonta* adventure
of staying to play late after school,
at a not-supposed-to-be-risky place.

This horrendous hideous accident,
a metal white soccer goal was not a friend,
but a merciless child assassin,
falling on top of its prey.

She is not here anymore!

And ...
I was there ...
Watching down from the patio,
she was thrown on the floor of the
humble community soccer court.
I watched her fight with death, and
I watched her losing the battle.

I was there ...
In the middle of the loudest silence
I have ever heard.
Seeing teachers scream, faint,
la desesperación to get help,
the crying,
taxis racing,

and like a *látigo de lightning*.
all in slow motion

And I was there ...

She is not here anymore!

I, in confusion,
in the deep of something so gray,
unnameable,
in the birth of an existential turmoil.

I was left floating in the immensity of the universe,
all by myself.,
While the innocent was marrying the unknown
and I could not be swallowed back into reality again.

I was kidnapped and thrown into the timeline of guilt.

She is not here anymore!

This little mighty girl
was not even seven yet,
but could control people's minds.
Ready to squeeze her opponent with a stomp.
Her personality must have been
too strong for the time she was born into.

Who was going to be my bloody competitor?
The rock in my school-aged shoe.
The one that ran behind me
and quietly pulled my ponytail,
so teachers wouldn't notice.
So they can still see her
as an innocent *palomita*.

Where did this girl go?
To hell or to heaven
I don't know.
My nemesis,
the carnivorous tiny flower in the school yard.

Who is going to give me headaches like her?
Annoying me to my core,
just to exercise her own power.
Who is going to pump up my creativity to avoid crossing paths
at the end of each class?

Who is going to challenge me like her?

I do not think there is anyone
who could ever take her place, ever.

I am sorry
our friendship could never flourish.

I am sorry
I did not cry for you
because you were my bully.

But I did not wish
for you to leave us so young,
and not like that.

You Left Me...

You were supposed to marry me.
but you left.
You left before
we could know each other better.

We walked together to school so many times.
You have now taken another road,
One, I can not follow, yet.

Forgive me because I did not send you my letter
when you were still at the hospital.
A *remolino* inside my heart did not allow me.
I could only see
that you left me here
and you went there, with the angels.

You never told me about your dreams,
but I was your best friend.
So, how could I not know them?

You loved to help others so much.
I could already see you in a doctor's robe
or as a social worker,
as a loving teacher, or as a father.
Those visions hurt the most.

Then, I just saw you as my pal at school.
But you were more than just my sidekick.
I remember you would follow my crazy ideas
just to be and play together.
We used to go to the other children's houses
to wake them up to go to school.
So little time, just with seven *primaveras*,
and I knew you and you knew me.

Some said that perhaps you paid your father's bill,
for his wrongdoings,
but why did I have to pay by losing you?

Forgive me, because I kept the letter to myself.

In the end, I was not strong enough to give it to you.
I did not want to let go of the last thing
that had your name.
It was going to mean more to me than to you.

What if grown ups could not make it get to your hands?
What if you could not read it?

That letter could accompany me until you got back to school.
But deeply, I was just avoiding the end
because I just knew
you were not going to come back.

I could only focus on
that somebody else would read
what was just meant for you.

¡Que tonta!
Now, you will never read it.
You won't get that hug, that flower, that word,
that love, just for you.
I could not say goodbye.

So young to leave.
But not so young to leave a mark in this world.
...In my world.

You meant the world to your parents,
and for someone else, too,
for me.

For me, you were my dear friend,
and maybe even something else.
You meant a *futuro*
and not only a past childhood love story.
You were a sweet nostalgia that lasted for many years
and I did not want to remember,
because I could never forget you.

I did not know if, then, I wanted to go with you.
I was keeping you here still in this invisible hole in my heart.
Many romantic relationships after you did not flourish.

Maybe because I was still waiting.

Today I finally can say,
Fly free as a hummingbird.
Go,
and maybe in another life,
I will marry you.

The Death of *Superniña*

It was the 90's in Lima, Peru,
and the highest point
of tabloid periodicals,

talking badly about women all the time,
showing their bodies on *vedettes*
almost naked on the front page,
and at the same time
other women and girls' bodies
raped and mutilated
without absolutely any embarrassment,
asesinamente sin vergüenza.
With comic strips to their back pages
where women asked for more sex
because they wanted to be mistreated.
Who were they trying to talk to?

Damn junk press, tabloid newspapers,
Estúpidos periódicos sensasionalistas.
The only thing ten year old me wanted
was reading,
being an informed citizen.
My biggest sin was wanting to know the news to learn,
saber del país.

Those inconsiderate beasts
set up the fire of my insecurities.
They groomed me towards self-doubt
and a toxic romantic life
as a future female adolescent and young woman.
Me, then an innocent young lady
could not even imagine the disaster
to which I have been seeded.

The brutal race of tabloid newspapers,
Prensa Chicha,
El mañanero, Ajá, Ojo, El grone, y muchos más

destroying the innocence of children,
only to sell more,

assassinating childhoods,
running them over.

I received all the bullets at the same time,
for being a voracious reader.

I believed I was the luckiest girl
for having all kinds of news to read
brought to me easily
by having access to the neighbor's newsstand.

I could come out of my cocoon
from serious newspapers
such as *Comercio and El Dominical.*
I could read what the majority read.
I did not know I was being a victim and witness
of the horrific graphic open first wave of femicide.
Bloodying my eyes and then my innocent tender soul.

And no one noticed
how *la superniña* in me was dying.
Como si a nadie le importara.

"Enlightenment/ iluminación,"
by Áurea María. Acrylic, 15x20 inches, 2016.

Father

Dad

I see you at the door,
waving your old hand
with your protruding veins
and slowly walking.

Dragging the discolored blanket of your years
constructed on top of our scarce family pictures,
lost forgotten treasures.
Those same pictures that hurt and make us smile,
and we wish we could have shared more.

You left with my childhood heart in your hands,
finally, uncovering the black holes in my past.
The same ones I did not want to see,
even though they were killing me
for so long…

and have followed me here,
to my own parenthood years.

I have looked for the answer *en tus silencios,*
but I could only find deeper sadness.
Our, moments that should have been
the happiest days of our lives.

My then-child's eyes could not understand.
I thought this pain was just my arrogance.
And this blame accompanied me
for so long…

It did not leave me alone.

So many years had passed.
Meanwhile, the Parkinsonian phantom
started to crawl inside you
quietly,
but quickly,
and started tearing apart your body.
A shadow began taking you over,
as a monster, it has not only eaten you

but also me
for so long...
so unbearable to see
that I can not take it anymore,
and I let it be.
It is now unleashed.

The only male hero
of my preschool years
is fading away.
Is leaving home.

I could not stand the grief then,
neither can I stand to see it now.
Como efecto colateral.
This feeling had been menacing me.
For so long...

I am trying to hold your hand,
but our contact has been weak.
For so long...

That even now
that finally
we both are trying.

Rrrrrr......pluck.

The pulling weight has separated
my last grasp from your hand,
that it became so normal
to detach,

to be apart was our thing,
but it did not cure anything.
It still hurts.
For so long...

For so long,
I was blinded, numbed,
kidnapped by everyday routines.

My closed head and heart
couldn't decode your quiet screams.
You, so vulnerable,
and me, still so hurt.

I cannot even remember anymore.
It is just a sorrowful chronic sensation.

You, so quiet, so far,
so unreachable to me.
I felt you gone already
before you were.

The pain is even more enormous now,
It devours me.
I fuss,
I crawl on the walls,
I want to talk but I can not.
The grief, as a *griffo*
stares me in the eye,
daring me to explode.

I can not surpass this
excruciating helplessness
of feeling fatherless already.
Even though you are seated here next to me,
and have been waiting for me to be here.
For so long...

But the pain is so dreadful.

My heart hurts
the world of each father and daughter's
relationship,
shiny or broken,
young or old,

the same one that nobody mentions
as if it does not matter.

I did not wish to anchor you to this world
while you're in such physical and emotional pain.

I just needed you for a little bit with me,
not for much longer,
just to be together,
and just be.

to reconnect
to heal,
to have real time,
to have real conversations.

To have just one day with you
where my childhood, teens, and adulthood
belong to the same life span,
dumping our masks of depression.

Inside the awareness that you were my father,
and I was not this fatherless orphan,
not like I have felt
for so long...

Maybe it was true,
my arrogance took your presence for granted.

I know you were going to leave,
somehow, I knew.
It was so scary,
to the bone.
...
But why must you go so early?
when I am just at the beginning of waking up.
I know,
you were waiting for me
For so long...

And I wish I could keep your last hug.
Pleno.
Free of those stains of fear.

So regret wouldn't following me
as a nostalgic ghost.
For so long...

And your last hug just stayed with me
forever,
moving through life and death.
...
Many moons have passed,
and my nightmare has become truth,
My stone heart in denial
has cracked
and has cried decades in just months.

I am not overdoing it,
as some seem to claim.
What can they claim from a daughter in horrendous pain?

I can not stop my crying
and just forget.

It is not their experience.
It is my pain,
my wound,
my relationship,

Mi padre,
just mine!

I want and need to disassemble my grief,
my trauma,
mi dolor,
rip it,
fragment it to its core.

Process it,
reattach it,
transform it,
to make amends with him,
and with myself to heal.

This is my pain!

I am not ashamed of feeling it anymore.
I do not have anything to lose.
I have lost it all already.
I will not be quiet, I won't!

Love your father,

not because he has shown you all his love.
He might have been absent,
even being there.
You do not know his complete story,
or the demons that he might have been fighting.

Love him,
because he is a person.
Forgive him,
just because he is your father!

To heal.
To love him.
To love yourself.
So you can love others.

Fighting The Bad Fight Again

I am fighting with God since he left me weakened.
After making me pay for my sins,
God fails by taking my father from me

I am dying without my father,
And now also without *Jesús*.
my friend from adolescence.
The only one who could put up with my stories,
and my sorrows.

The only one who didn't judge me for being a young tasteless girl
without glory in high school.

I'm fighting with my friend.
And now,
who am I going to turn to
or whose hand am I going to hold onto?
in my hardest times?

Little by little,
I need to regain confidence.
Rely.

I can't lose my other father too.

Sorry

i want to say sorry,
to all those women whose fathers left.
i did not pay attention to their pain.

i tell them sorry,
But in reality,
i want to say sorry to myself.
Because i did not learn from their pain in time.
They were trying to teach me how crucial
it is to stop and analyze our relationships.

That a father is much more than blood.
They were trying to teach me with their stories,
even when they did not know me.

i want to say sorry,
because i did not lower my fences
to allow me to feel their pain
before i was kidnapped and trapped by this tremendous pain,
mi propio carcelero.
That has robbed me of the chance of experiencing my father.

i want to say sorry,
because i did not allow myself to love my own father
Having him at home.
When so many girls didn't have that.

i could not forgive him for things
that had nothing to do with me.

i was carrying and feeding those *rencores*
that my mother, my grandmother,
my aunts planted in me
y anidé equivocadamente
deep inside me.

With invisible hands as *tentáculos*
they seeded them on my back
and i incorporated them

without realizing their toxicity.

i want to say sorry,
because i was carrying *esta angustia,*
este dolor,
not mine to bare
and i
i cared so much to keep it that way.
i could not comprehend why.

It became a black flower,
the one i still am.

Ellas raised crows in my own chest
that almost took my eyes out.
Y lo más triste
is that they didn't know
how it could damaged me.

i am sorry,
to my child because
yo tampoco me curé a tiempo
i did not resolve the hole in my heart
before he was born,

And i should've.
And i really tried.
But i did not really have an idea how immense
the neglected grief was.
And me being hurt,
i hurt him.

i am sorry,
because
i was unaware of the severity of my own issues.
también
did not help to heal their hearts.

The older women in my family
were waiting for my actions,
I don't want to leave the same heavy toxic
inheritance.

but how to break this intricate chain
sin quedar completamente rota?

And at the same time,
they and i have perpetuated the hurt,
the wound already.
...

And where was his heart left,
my dad's heart?
And what about his hugs?

i am sorry,
because i did not appreciate that small step he took,
he hugged me and i refused to hug him back
strong and open, and
I should have.
It just hurt too much.
So unbearable to breathe, to speak,

to love.
Just like dying.
Just like trying to not give birth.

i say sorry,
to my child because he is a boy
and when i thought i had already learned
to not hate men,
my progress was just not enough.

My stupid gullibility,
though i was already a progressive minded woman,
but i just had made a small patch on the surface
as an ignorant person does.
And i dragged my child to the hole of my own void.

Ancestral healing is a lifelong learning process
that goes further than a lifetime.
Maybe his grandchild will be free *de esta cruz*

i am sorry,
because i am also leaving my line of pain in our family tree,

because I keep cutting them,
deplumándolas,
yo misma.

i am sorry,
because i don't want to let go of my father's hand,
when he wants me to fly high.
i did not understand then,
his pain did not let him talk,
he was telling me that he loved me then and now.

In the way of silence,
i want to fly to honor him,
but my wings are too heavy, tired, and almost broken.

i am sorry,
finally,
i am conscious of our pain.
i am tired
and trying as you were.
i am sorry
Papá.

One can only know
when you become a parent

I Was...

Me, the son you never had
to fill up the hole in your heart.
I was a little girl playing to be the savior,
to set sail and move our family towards a safe port,
to feel I was worthy enough of your attention
and maybe even pride.

I was pretending so much to be strong
and so confident,
as your son would have been,
that I became so weak,
that a paper could hold much more pain than me.

I was the one getting your gifts of baggie clothes
all red, meant for a boy,
with enormous tennis shoes,
chancabuques.
No wonder why I became self-conscious
I, so strongly, felt what I had to do.

I was the girl, expecting to fit the size,
the strength and the outlook,
of somebody I was not,
your son.

I was the dragon himself,
No man could dare to look me in the eye.
Dressed in red as the fire,
just trying to protect myself
from my own risk taker initiative.
Putting a fence between the danger
and my supposed *valentía.*
Por lo visto me salió mal.

I didn't even know how mad I was.
My eyes in the mirror one day told me.

I was the son you never had and you did not know it.

But
I was not your son
yo era tu hija!

Y sigo siendo tu hija,
Even though you are not here anymore.

Yo soy tu hija todavía,
Papá.

*"We did not forget our mother's forced sterilizations/
No hemos olvidado las esterilizaciones forzadas de nuestras madres"
by Áurea María. Charcoal, 15x20 inches, 2016.*

Society

No! al olvido y la injusticia

Ni con el paso de los años y estaciones,
ni el cambio de gobierno,
ni siquiera con el cambio de nuestros nombres.
¡No vamos a olvidar!

No vamos a olvidar el entierro del dolor
de nuestras madres,
por la sociedad, las leyes, y todos.

De sus sueños
por algún día ser madres nuevamente.
Aunque fuera una elección con decisión,
imperfecta o no,
una que nunca tomarán.
Era su decisión.
Les arrancharon el único valor real
de la mujer en las provincias de la sierra.
a los ojos del patriarcado andino,
dar a luz.

Me reflejo en sus lágrimas.
Mujeres del mundo parcialmente desdibujadas,
ultrajadas en sus cuerpos y derechos,
mujeres tradicionales que soñaron ser madres
de varios hijos
desde casi que tiene uso de razón,
robadas de sus sueños.

"Qué más da si sólo son unas pobres mujeres,
a quienes les ayudaron a planificar mejor su familia".
Claro, y los tiranos dirán eso
Y ellas, sin pedirlo, sin quererlo, sin saberlo,
como si fuera un juego!
Fueron por ayuda y la mutilación de su fertilidad fue su pago.

Ellas ya no podrán dar más sucesores,
"más mano de obra," como algunos dicen,
hombres del campo tampoco perdonan.
Y así,

unos mirándolas por debajo del hombro por tener más hijos,
y otros cortando sus pequeñas alas por no poder tener más,
aunque quisieran.

Claro,
como siempre la mujer no puede ganar,
Y menos las pobres y de color.
Doblemente pisadas,
quizás hasta triplemente olvidadas.

Que les importó a esos, disque doctores,
esterilizar sin ton, ni son,
encaprichados de poder
sobre unos úteros que ellos no tienen.
Por el asqueroso dinero o un sólo favor político,
jugando a ser Dios,
o el monstruo puppet master de la natalidad.
Que con su pincel maquiavélico bisturí,
enmascaraban las manos de la eugenesia,
en nombre de la mejora de vida de los países,
sólo no permitiéndoles nacer,
truncando la vida fértil de sus madres.
Borrándolas.

Pues ahora están más presentes,
ellas en nosotras,
en la marcha
Esta generación de mujeres;
hijas, sobrinas, nietas de ellas
es su voz perdida,
sonando,
pisando fuerte.

¡Escúchalas!

Nadie podrá ya jugar con úteros,
que no son suyos,
ni esterilizar sus voces
porque ahora tienen
mujeres guardianes
conscientes de sus derechos
para defenderlas.

No! to oblivion and injustice

Not even with the passing of the years and seasons,
nor the change of government,
not even with the change of our names,
we will not forget!

We will not forget the buried pain
of our mothers,
by society, the laws, and everyone.

Of their dreams
to someday become mothers again,
Even if it was a decisive choice,
imperfect or not,
it was one they will never take.
Era su decisión.
They ripped away the only real value
of a woman in the mountain provinces.
In the eyes of the Andean patriarchy,
giving birth.

I see myself in their tears.
Women of the world partially blurred,
violated in their bodies and rights,
traditional women who dreamed of being mothers
of many children
since they were little girls,
stolen from their dreams.

"What difference does it make if they are poor women,
who were forcibly sterilized to help plan their family better."
Of course, the tyrants will say that!
And they did it to these women, without asking for it, without wanting
it, without knowing it,
As if it were a game!
These women went for help and mutilation of their fertility was their
payment.

They will no longer be able to have more successors,
"more hands for labor," as some say.
The men of the countryside do not forgive "flaws" either.

And then,
some looking down on them for having more children,
and others cutting their little wings because they couldn't have more,
even if they wanted to.

Of course,
As always, the woman cannot win,
And even less the poor and colored ones.
Stepped on twice,
and forgotten three times.

What do those people care about, so called doctors,
sterilize *sin ton, ni son,*
infatuated with power
against the wombs that they do not have.
For disgusting money or only political favor,
playing God,
or the monster puppet master of birth.
That with his Machiavellian scalpel brush,
masked the hands of eugenics,
in the name of improving the lives of countries,
just not allowing them to be born,
truncating the fertile lives of their mothers.
Deleting them.

Well, now, they are more present,
them in us,
on the march
This generation of women:
their daughters, nieces, granddaughters.
It's their lost voice
Sounding,
Stepping strong.

Escúchalas!

No one will be able to play with uteruses anymore,
that are not theirs,
nor sterilize their voices
because now they have
guardian women
aware of their rights
para defend them.

My Own Soap Opera

I recollect now,
the fruits of my childhood
surrounded by TV and romantic sad songs.

Channel five,
8 pm, *hora punta,*
flying dishes through the windows,
by sobbing women on my screen
not fighting their feelings anymore
and letting it be...
but yes,
fighting for the love
from someone undeserving of their pain.

The TV is leaking into my town.
The neighborhoods in the starring paper,
while my mother is just cooking
some more *caldo de gallina.*
A scoop of just some more salty drama,
sorry, I wanted to say
just some more ground cumin and garlic.

>   What a stupid life,
>   those women suffer *por las puras*!
>   *Sí, sí,* Momma.
>   *Son tontas.*
>   Of course, I would never do that.

Oh, child,

you don't know yet
the *alcances* of watching soap operas
at such a young age.

--

A soap opera,
written and played in the 2020's,
is now running its episodes,
written with hopes,

but badly played

disque with adult decisions,
and many times worse, edited.
But sometimes,
the actors try to remedy them,
you could say.

They are just kidding in their attempt.
It just makes the issue worse and bigger.
With not enough knowledge of themselves,
Of how to fix it?

Is this *telenovela* recording pure prejudice
left by the ancestors to be fixed
supposedly a gift?

Well, a raw gift, I guess.

But we listened with wrong ears,
misunderstood our inheritance.
Treasure already set, I said,
that I used to my convenience
in the plot of my very own destruction.

Sabotaje comes very easy,
In the hands of the hurt,
don't you know?

A novela that seems comical sometimes

but it is just absurd.
Punching the same storylines,
over and over again.

Little drama, big drama,
sneaky egos,
silence as way of talking,
lies wanting to quiet truths,
jealousy coming out as contempt.
Dismissive as the best way of taking action,

letting your trauma dominate the scene,

All this miscommunication
disguised as romantic.

Time is rolling too fast,
I can feel the crash
of my very own destructive narrative arch,
the illusion is behind..

This novela is not winning me over,
Not now that I took off my denial glasses.

I confront it.
It should not fulfill its destiny,
Because I better know better,
with no other choice
than to rediscover myself for the first time.

Because of social construction,
loyalty is not given,
Más bien acaso, an assassin.
And I better do better,
and just allow myself to shine .
I owe it to my misled ancestry line,
In this post Covid daily life.

I've survived physically and emotionally
using something greater than the same old script.

I am the creator and the star of my own story.
I have the power of
casting,
hiring,
and if needed,
firing people in my life.

Producing and directing my future is on me.

I am the shaper of my destiny.

Female Legs Should Live Without Fear

Wearing pants stands for empowerment,
Not always in my Latin America!
It is changing, but my teen years have seen it all.

My contained frustration screamed a *solas*;

I'm sick of having to take care of my skirt from creeps
since my very early teens,
because my body just dares to be
in the early growth range.

I am fed up with wearing pants
as public chastity underpants,
so I can just scream to the world
don't trespass here!

That I have to scrap pieces of my self-esteem's skin
in exchange for just more basic safety.
It is just insultingly diminishing!

That I cannot calm my mind of
being careful about my surroundings
allll the timeee,
todo el tiempo,
and focus on living life.

East, west, and even south
can be dangerous in each turn over.
That only the north can be safer.
Even immigration plays the same role.

If you don't watch out enough,
each day on the bus,
on the market,
on the street,
your intimate clothing parts
that only belong to you
can finish in a sinister pervert's phone.

Why have I had to talk
with a hoarse gangster type masculine voice?

So much so to the point
that I began to question my own gender?
All just to scare away
the chasing shadowy hands coming to my school skirt,
that is *disque*
and naughty.

It is like if the crazy lunatic is saying to me,

"You crazy lunatic.
I am just being nice to you.
You should like it!"
It is your morbid desires.
I am getting used to dealing with it,
and that is even worse, scary...

I can not trust any guy at all, young or old.
It doesn't matter if you are pretty, average, or just a child.

Follow the rules, lady!
Or you will pay for being too dumb.
And if you did not allow their crap for fear,
be ready, they will just scream at you
stupid, *zorra* or *puta*!

Do not talk to any guy that way
because only whores do that.

How did we get here?
When did a smile became an invitation to rape?
As if they are being told,
    "Come here, I am available.
    I have been waiting for you!"

How has this become the second reason for leaving my country,
only after education and work, how?
Isn't it our right to live without the basic fear of an assault?
I am here, I am safe for now.
It is an illusion that I hope lasts a lifetime.

At the north,
My skirts are ecstatic for going out, finally.
And finally, my thighs rediscovered the cool breeze

my legs were already tired of being unnaturally light and locked up.

They missed the sun's hug.

The breeze of autumn smells like freedom!

          So, take away your insulting preying gaze from my legs,
              All the nightmares easily start out like that!

                        They are only mine.

I am here in my new house,
I won't leave this one.

If we wear pants,
it must be by choice,
for comfort,
for practicality,
or styling,
not as armor,
or as a barrier for protection.

Let legs be free in the south or the north,
East or west let them be part of the world,
just as they are,
a part of the body.

One More Newborn Girl

My friend cried when her daughter was born.

> But what is wrong, my dear?
> "It's a girl, it's a girl," she said,
> while her joyful voice cracked.
> A shadow of sadness *se sentó*
> next to her and her newborn.

I could hear it in her voice without saying,
and see it in her eyes
she knew she was condemned to see her baby girl
enslaved by invisible *cadenas*
perpetrated by society starting soon.

As if this baby girl already had a mark on her forehead,
that said she will endure the weight of the world
on her *hombros,*
That she was destined to feel pain in her *caderas*
not only for giving birth,
but because boys will say she is only worth
the size of her curves.

Some decades ago,
being judged by the world
for having hips too wide.
Now, for having them too narrow.

The world of fashion,
style,
men's desires,
economy,
society,
do not care about the body
of the everyday women.

We are real women.

They just feast on women's
insecurities,
just to make money

taking the most advantage of them that they can.

Most of them are never pleased
and never will be,
and we do not have to please them.

Even though the world teaches us
since we are very young,
we are supposed to be born to please.

Even though we still live in a world of contradiction
and the most infuriating truth is that the worst judgments
will come from other women's mouths

from
a lady neighbor,
a mother-in-law,
a sister-in-law,
a friend,
a sister,
and worst,
our very own mother,

If we, women, can not understand our pain and struggle,
who will?

      "My poor baby!" she said.

A mother should not,
must not cry for the birth of one more woman to be.

This *bebita* should be seen
for what she really is,
a diamond,

the hope,

the next great engineer,
scientist, doctor, lawyer, astronaut,
artist, philosopher, teacher,
even perhaps the next *Presidenta*.

A newborn girl
the woman of the future.

What a Latino Woman Is Supposed to Be

I can not cook the great Peruvian dish
to provide for your cookouts,
I can not teach you recipes from my grandma.
I am neither sexy or motherly.
Not that I haven't tried,
it is just not my natural flow.
That does not mean that I can not be when I want to.
When I feel like I can,
but that is not your choice.
It is mine.

I am somewhat masculine, some say.
I am that part that my father could not be, I guess.
And it's ok now, I have accepted that part of me,
I had to be the man of my family home,
and I am happy
I was able to be that then,
when I thought my family needed it.

I had to become a feminist,
to not lose my feminine side.
Or more because I did not want to be *la víctima*.
I did not want to be a woman waiting for her man at the house,
waiting for him to decide,
or to say what or how things have to be done.

Not living really,
but almost dying just for her children.
Being a ghost, zombie of the household chores.
But maybe deep inside me, maybe I did.
But it is ok, it is not your problem.
It is mine. I will figure it out.

It's just me.
I am Latina,
I am a woman.
One of a kind,
not too traditional or modern.
Not too quiet and not too loud.
Not always smiling and not always pleasing.

Or maybe the opposite,
when I have to be.
Sorry, and not sorry
if I disappointed your expectations
of the label you were trying to put on me.

I might be caught in the transitions,
lost in translation,
and even stuck in the intergenerational trap.
I am not that usual reference of Latina
you have heard of.
Don't put me in a box,
No me encasilles.
I am only trying my best to be me.

I only know this way.
Even though I already wasted my time
trying to change for others,
and hurt myself,
denying who I truly am.

I know who I am now
a mother, a daughter,
a sister, a friend,
a Spanish native speaker,
a Latino woman—
una Latina.
And not only a woman,
but human.

So, back off and let me be.

¡Y vive tu vida,
mientras yo vivo la mía!

Sentenced or Not?

How much have our dads really marked us as failures
in our future love life?
Why did I choose a man who was unavailable?
What dragged me here.
A ésta, mi historia.

Like a little girl dragging the dirty laces
of her worn dress all around the house,
while holding onto an old doll.
She didn't seem to know
she has been dragging the long old laces for a while,
but still is very attached to them.

The laces tied to her, now, broken wrists are hurting
but she just doesn't care,
or just doesn't want to see.
She just keeps pulling those laces like its familiar,
just hurting herself a little bit more.

Occasionally
running, stopping suddenly,
stepping on the lace,
almost on purpose,
sobbing for a second and trying to keep playing.
Como si nada.

The only thing left is a sordid smell of emptiness.

Was I dragging my sorrows or his? or ours?
Maybe, it was not even my nostalgia, but just inherent family
loyalty to pain.

Is this the real purpose of your childhood?
Or your life?

And what about your adult love life?

My dad was there but really not present.
His love was there
but it did not flow through me.

Like having everything,
but locked in a metal see-through safe,
without a key.

So you could see the treasure from close
not able to access it,
and be left to just starve of the love
unconsciously denied.

When are you going to stop to really look at yourself,
little girl and let go of your pain?

You are grown now,
You have more power now.
See yourself, mírate,
in the mirror of your own time
but now, in the present

And you?

Who really has been pulling the laces
then?
Who is pulling the laces now?

Our Very Own People

How did I not realize who my very own people were until very
late in life?
Perhaps even until it was too late to give them the love they
deserved,
Maybe because my own family did not know how to love their
own people either.

It broke me just to learn.
The way of loving our own family has been dull, dismissive,
and passive like if our attachments would be meaningless.
Where has the trauma taken us?

I used to love learning so much,
but now learning to strip our faults
and voids from their disguise
gives me this resonant sordid pain.

Trying to escape this pain is not a cure.

Just give up,
rendirse completamente.
Traveling to the wounds is the only answer to grow,
to start the life I am meant to live.

It hurts to finally understand that other people could wait,
but not my very own people.
And they have waited for so long already.

When they hurt,
when they struggle,
when they do not find the way to make their voices work,
when they cry,
sometimes we tell them they need to handle it themselves,
all alone, because we are busy,
overwhelmed,
always living for others
outside of our home.
Now that I opened my eyes,
I see the figure of my son and my parents
as I never seen them before.

Even now that my father is gone,
now he is finally closer to me.
Many times,
we want to become *"gente buena,"*
helping, listening,
pleasing all others first.
But what about our own families?

Sometimes,
I think this is a Latino thing.
So sad to see the dark side,
the dark reality of my own culture.
Slavery perhaps has not finished
putting its finger in our wounds yet.
It is the only explanation
for this recurrent nightmare.

...But now I can see, it does not happen in functional families.

Sorry, mom and dad,
now I understand,
maybe what you could not then.
I made you be an outsider in my life,
and honestly you do not know me well yet.
You do not know my real dreams and pain.

I don't know you well either.
Neither the gifts you or I have,
we didn't recognize them in each other.
What a waste!

It is hard to believe the saying "it's never is too late."
Está demasiado trillado.
But when you fell in the hole
of the no hope, *sin esperanza,*
the only thing to do is to fall further into a deeper hole.

Letting it consume you and overtake you.

Maybe we can still save some love between us, mom,
to be the family I have been longing for.
Even though dad is gone, and he can not feel any
happiness, but gladly no more pain either.
Surpassing fates of religion, in spirituality,
maybe he can still feel our attempt to redeem ourselves.

Sorry, to my dear son,
because without realizing,
and against my will,
I have been serving to perpetuate this ancestral wound
and it has caught your childhood.
I have been doing the same to you.
Repeating the very same pattern
I have condemned my parents for.

With this awareness,
"I will do better."

They Are Looking At You. Are They Only Dishes?

And here they are,
hanging around like nothing,
like they own the space.
THEY, the dirty plates in the sink,
looking at me,
haughty and sometimes *condescendientes*,
judging me, *escrutiniando* my faults.

As if they will be at their own home.
With their stains, *todos aplastados*,
but still as they would not have their own secrets,
as they would be perfect,
trying to convince me to let go and give up,
trying to materialize my husband's voice each time.

Our fight is continuous,
for what?
Now, I know...
Just to waste time...

To sabotage our souls one more time,
to make us pay *lo que le debemos a la vida*.

Each day the battle starts in the early morning.

It will only end the day that I do not give the dishes the power.
I know.
And I know, I know,
but maybe my heart doesn't understand yet.

> Do not look back at them.
> Just keep walking your own path,
> *hasta que sea tuyo* and you believe it.
> *Y venga de ti.*

The Other Perspective
(Part 2 - Coming From "They Are Looking At You")

They are waiting all puzzled
for me? For what?
To solve them?

The dishes are just there.
Just showing how they are,
just resting,
descansando a pata estirada,
laying there,
in the middle of feeling contempt and overwhelmed.

Just not minding
or bloody needy, just like themselves,
en precaria condición.
Maybe, it does not matter how or why.
But what do they want from me?

Who am I to them?
Why do they do this to me?
I am not their mother
they are not my child,
or are they?

Why do they make my heart hurt?
What is missing?
Or what am I missing?

Are they just dishes?
How do they have so much power over me?
And further,
do I have some power over them
or some power at all?

Why am I crushed,
como está mi corazón?
Maybe they are just asking for...
Me... to be

the decider, the doer,
la mujer o el hombre.

Ah!
Maybe I get it now,
and I better know now,
or they will be there
until I have the strength.
The strength that is somewhere inside
mí mísma.

Until... I let it all just flow as it should be,
let the light enter in my mind
the warmth in my heart,
and I hug myself!

When I can embrace myself as,
who I really am,
those dishes will know.
and they will rest,
and they will be just what they are
Platos.

"The Scream of my Inside" by Áurea María charcoal over paper, 20x15 inches.

Relationships

Loving A Vulnerable Sincere Woman

It has to hurt,
If you are not prepared for her,
for her voice,
her unconventional way of being.
Doesn't it?

Because
She will tell you her most intimate fears.
She will talk about her more challenging dreams,
sus sueños de niñez, *o del futuro,*
her daily invisible fights to surpass her traumas,
and everyday problems,
que ya es lo de menos.

You might get intimidated
by all she is holding inside.

You just have to let her
handle her demons,
hold her hand
and still handle your own life.

It may look like a cross at first,
but it's actually a gift from God.
You have to be able to see
further than the surface,
of your love for her.

It is not known if you deserve it,
or if you are ready
for so much love
overflowing.

Choose well
whether to open your door
to her love or not.

She will be a rollercoaster of emotions
until you shelter her,

taking her by the hand

and little by little
she will land in a world
more stable,
more balanced.

You just have to know how to love her
y ya!

She will love you
like never before,
with vulnerability and the sincerity you have been afraid of,
but you must take care of her first
para también ser amado.

especially in those vulnerable moments,
Un amor sinceramente retribuido,
entero.
es solo lo que quiero.

Against time

Missed beats.
Destiempos.
Untimely.

Our story began against time.
Against my own timeline and yours.
Without respect for our own cycles,
immaturity and loneliness pushed us
to take shelter together
when we weren't ready yet.

Overwhelmed with my fears and their shadows,
I didn't let you into my heart.
And when I was able to open my eyes,
you didn't allow me to enter yours.

The constant dance of missing the beat
does not stop
Now, we have danced it so shamefully,
with eyes closed and eyes open
for just too long.
That I am just too sick,
tan mareada, confundida.
It just hurts too much
to even dare to stop.

The missed beats in our hearts,
sewn by your sour words
have exacerbated my wounds.
And my hurt has hurt not only your pride.

I, your weakness,
on the wrong side of love.
My hollow demands,
my debilitating company,
my irritable voice that just leads to
your trauma on fire.
Me, the guilty,
maldita bruja desgraciada,
la que te hace hacer estas cosas.

in your more sane moments,
when you finally decide
to give me the gift of your word,
much better
than your extortionistic silent treatment.

===

After a while, I thought I had recovered.
Did I really recover?
Mi autoestima dónde está?

Maybe we never will recover completely again.
Life came back to normal,
but is it normal?

If you came back to be the same way
from before,
I could not tell.
I was too lost
in the midst of this mismatched relationship.

Mi ventana cerrada,
you could not reach me.
Mostly because
I saw you as *mi verdugo.*
Your sporadic flashes of light could not illuminate,
nor warm my heart.

Our story,
our *caminos,*
our time together
has already been torn so much
that the little love left here
fell through the holes of the tears.

There is almost nothing here,
not enough support, care, or intimacy as true friends.
It is better to preserve what remains,
to survive both,
until we can figure out
to see if this intricate love
is worth saving.

Maybe in another life
our efforts,
conscience,
and values
line up
and match our time,

y pueda florecer el amor.

Sólo que en ésta, no.

The Most Imperfect Of the Two Of Us

Lower your voice, calm down!
I have heard what you said.
You do not need to scream.
Contrary to what you seem to think of me,
it is not how I understand.

I am being real when I say
I am the most imperfect of the two of us.
Possibly I am the most imperfect
person in the entire world.

Not as you said,
not the worst of the worst,
like the waste of your time,
the lowest of women ever,
Or dismissive on purpose
just to hurt you.

ni la mas tonta,
ni una mujer sin corazón.

Finally, after a lot of damage
I had to learn to dodge your venom.
I had to learn in order to survive.
In order to just be me.

===
I am the most imperfect,
¡y qué!

I have holes and an abyss,
of voids, depressions,
rocky lands
in my confidence,
validated by your critical words
especially when fallen.

I have lakes,
no sólo lagunas en mi memoria,
and that is how I forget

our dysfuntionality, sometimes.

Yes, sure, my mountains of nonsense are there
"for not seeing your great effort."

I know, your glasses can only see what is perfect.

I am made up of confused *wanna* be correct feelings,
suppressed wishes and opinions,
tied up, *amordazados* by this dysfunctional cycle we are in,
screaming oppressed out of the box ideas kept silent,
and a load of not so happy and happy mistakes.

I am also defined by my passion for my work.
I have the constant debilitating regrets of leaving my child
in the care of others to go to chase my passion,
helping other children on their paths.

It might not make sense to you
or even to myself,
but it fills me up,
even when I could be a bit broken on the inside.

I have to hold my breath when taking chances,
when deciding,
I am not as sharp,
clear,
and smart
as you keep telling me to be.

Now, I finally understood what you meant,
but your unnecessary rough ways tell me a
different story.
They scratch my soul,
don't you see it?

I won't follow your directions,

B E C A U S E,

it is my own person,
just me,

who should tell me
in what direction I should go.

I don't know how,
but I still have some energy left to survive, to continue,
but not for the nonsensical fight with your perfectionism,
that has already got us stuck in this mud of negativity.
I won't deal with it anymore.

There is no more time to lose
I need to start living.

           Maybe it's too late for "us,"
           but maybe there is still time
           to try to not be so perfect
           in order to just really "be,"
           ourselves separately.

The Final Battle

Your daily
"I don't want to hear your voice anymore,"
is so angrily sincere and full of rage,
that it comes to me like a savage wave,
wiping me out from myself.
So much that
I do not want to talk anymore.

A voiceless spiral of unworthiness
is taking over my personality
my me being me is going to be gone soon
if I can not let out the thoughts in my mind
into the world.

Don't you see?
You are drilling a deeper wound
in the heart of this already decayed relationship.

With freshly anger pouring from your eyes,
you have burnt me on purpose.
Just to hear my silent cries.

I wish I could be your worst enemy right now.
I wish I could exchange places with your enemy,
and feel at least some compassion
because for you he is still human,
yes,
but not me.

Any minimal outburst from me starts the fire of your anger and my
trauma.

Like a time bomb ticking in my ear,
your resonant steps,
followed by your high pitch yell
starts the frenetic alarm.

Danger is all I can hear.

My body's reaction is so offensive to you
that my worst sin is to just feel.

I feel closer each time to the fangs of fear.
Playing with my hair,
breathing in my ear,
so much that
I can not feel anymore.
I am numb, *sedada*,
Ya es demasiado.

I am just like that worn piece of paper
that you try to rip out of your diary on a daily basis.
Blown by the air,
feeling so light,
in a timeless sordid meadow,
just ready to fall.

You have snatched me from myself.
Yes, you did,
finally your plan has succeeded.
You might be happy at last.

I was my last treasure,
my last resource.
Y ahora qué?
Is it our end only?
Or also my end?

No!
It is the end of the silence of my voice!

Most Powerful Resource

Face my vulnerability with a sword if you like,
as you usually do,
I can't control that
but if you still care,
bring some repairing tools with you as well
to cover my hurt with a blanket after the battles

But before the last possibility of reconsideration, a pause
Before I continue,
I should re-read the promise
I was about to break
to that roaring little girl
with a very well done ponytail.

--No crying for any man,
        only if it is your dead father or your son.
--Never lose your voice.

Remember little girl
you are not your last resource
You are your most precious resource
and the most powerful..

Bring out your power
And
Exercise your voice!

And if you do not accept my voice
there is No deal.
This is not negotiable.

The Violence Of Your Silence

It has touched my deepest fibers.
You know how I hate
not knowing about anything for very long,
and how hard it is for me
still to speak up,
rogar por atención.

The lash of your silent communication
creates miscommunication
you know
an invisible gap
that might never cure.

It's like a betrayal to my sensitivity.
You know,
that I am like a flower with fragile petals
but strong roots in the deep of me.

I thought that maybe my secure place was you,
but I am just realizing
it only can be in me.
Only in me.

The violence you are allowing
to drop into my soul,
I won't receive it anymore.
Esto ya no te lo dejaré pasar.

It won't drag me to hell again.
It is double jeopardy.
You know I have survived already
the death of myself.
I won't lose myself again.

It hurts to love you
and not love you.
But I will put myself first this time

and forever.

It is me,
who leaves you.

Sadly but firmly,

your loss.
is my win.

Where Is ...

...all that love I denied you?

Where is the deprivation that I brought you?

I did not know
I made you feast on insecurities and *vacío*,
yours, mine,
ya no importa.
I did not know that
by protecting myself from being hurt,
I have hurt you.

I did not know you had stuffed your pain so deep inside,
tan dentro that,
I could not hear your cry even in a lifetime.
Worst, if I hadn't learned to listen to myself yet.

All I have heard all this time is
"I hate you."
Not from your mouth at first,
but from your actions
that were screaming louder
y cada vez más fuerte
to my face,

with your,
I don't have time,
I won't help you,
I don't want to go anywhere,
I don't have time, not for you!
I don't want to go anywhere,
not with you!

And your silent treatment screamed
so horribly at me.

mad,
raging,
deformed,
screeching,

splatter,
static,
numbed.

I didn't feel human anymore.

I had not felt human for a while.

Now, we are far from our hands, ears,
and much further from our hearts,
even though sometimes we are at the same table,
we have been invisible to each other.

Ya, it is too late,
Ya pasamos la línea.

I always wonder why I allow it,
I always wonder why at some point
I accepted and believed I deserved it.

Maybe it's because
my subconscious felt it had to be paid back
for the pain I caused you.

I broke you inside *sin querer*,

I guess you were also broken already.
I did not like that petrifying sadness in your eyes,
disculpa. It scared me.

But when you broke my person as you did,
you did, in fact, force me
not only rediscover
but discover who I really am.

It Is Me,

I only discovered how deep I had hurt you
because I decided to embrace this hurt
as a dear child, born from me,
and live it in my own way

I tasted the pain,
wrapped myself in it,
rediscover its meaning
as reading the same book
but with a new perspective.
Going from the end to the beginning,
and involving myself in this path.
Not allowing differences between
el camino y yo misma.

And it's not you,
And it's not only me,
And it's not only you,
It is we,
but it is me.

Me, who has to,
needs to,
wants to evolve,
transform--meditate
my trauma.

Even though I have tried
to pay for
what I didn't really know I did to you,
I have to pay more for
the sabotage I did to myself.

I need to pay it by picking me up,
caring and standing up again.

It is really me and only me.

Sé que soy yo,
Quien debe dar el paso.
La solución está en mis manos.
Todo es para y por mi
y para mi bienestar
y mi felicidad.

I am who I am...

Don't tell me I have to be a strong woman,
that, that's how I have to be,
with that voice between order and complaint.

No me digas como ser yo!

I want to be when I feel it
when I want it.
Not because you
tell me,
ask me,
beg me, or
impose it on me.

Let me be,
speak,
think for myself.
Breathe...

I feel like I'm drowning.

Sometimes I am strong,
Sometimes I'm not.
Sometimes I'm like a dove.
And you feel sorry for her.
Why?

I am her, I am a dove.
Don't tell me how to be.
Hasta me quieres decir como ser paloma.

I am a butterfly or a dove.
Revoloteando vivo,
and that is how I love.

Don't worry about me.
I am living life, I am flying my journey.
Mi transformación.

I'm not asking
you to worry so much that it steals your peace,
I am just feeling fragile,
maybe vulnerable.
And what?
Let me feel.

Sometimes I'm like lightning that cuts chains in its path.
A force that devastates you, because you want to see that.

Finally,
I have learned to be
how I want to be when I want,
This flower in me was born
from the crying and the strength
of my inner little girl that I lost inside my fears.

You can't come to take away what I am.
Y borrarme.
You won't do it. I won't allow it.
Because if you get in the way of me being me
one day I'll have to step over you.

I will fly like the dove that I am.
Vulnerable or strong
when I decide.

Remember,
you are only an observer, not my tamer.
Enjoy me while I am here.
Because if you throw stones at me,
you won't be able to see me anymore in your sky.

I decide in which sky I fly.

Enjoying the Flaws

I need to be with
somebody who enjoys me.

Somebody that appreciates my spontaneity,
not taking it as just dumb nonsense,
Somebody perceptive enough to be open to finding
its whimsical side.
Su magia.

Somebody that enjoys the journey of how my brain works,
a beautiful labyrinth that teaches me
how to get lost,
questioning my own self, and
to find my own answers by and for myself.

Somebody that can see further than the forms
and the social perfectionism,
with an open mind and understanding of my intentions
Somebody who wants to work it out with me.

Somebody that doesn't judge me for taking the side road
sometimes,
and just walks next to me by freedom of choice.
Sólo por su propio gusto.

Somebody who feeds and adds to my vision.
Somebody who wants to ride this bumpy ride
called life. *conmigo,*
Somebody that can dream those dreams with me
de la mano.

Somebody that can read me without translation,
in any language,
even in the language of loving silence,
and wants to create with me
our very own language for ourselves.
No matter the issue we are talking about,
understand each other.

I need the flaws inside me

and the functioning of my mind,
to piece together my soul
like something imperfect that is.

It needs the fractures, cracks,
hendiduras, rajaduras,
to breathe,
to feel...

Perfection would just destroy me...

An understanding without trying to understand,
a world in your hands,
and your eyes without effort to read me.
Fluidez simplemente.

Maybe I will die
without living this love story.
Or maybe I will just live an incomplete love story.
But I, at least, have lived life as it came
which is fully in my eyes,
even if it was for just a moment.

I have lived it with all its flaws.
For that I had to see them as flowers instead.
And it was a beautiful imperfection.

So, take me as I am,
with my broken edges,
my transitory nightmares,
my anxiety questioning often or sometimes.

Learn to love my spontaneity
not only because it comes with the package,
but because it enhances the sudden opportunities of freedom
that we are, sometimes,
a gift from the universe.

Learn to see it with new shades.
A new direction will let you appreciate this way,
my way of seeing things,

will let you appreciate me
and love me
how I deserve

Love Me Like I Was Gone Already

Si de veras quieres una oportunidad.

Love me in the present,
like if you would be longing for me already,
so we can create the best in you and me,
So we can flourish
right now,
before it is too late.

Love me as if I would be here just for a day.
and then, I will go to war.
Love me like that,
and we will discover what we are made of.
Our real souls will finally talk.

Together, as before I left the country
and you suffered from your knee pains.
Before I made myself a slave of monotony,
before you found my flaws so disgusting
and unbearable.

See in me,
ese misterio
that attracted you
at the beginning.
Keep and feed this love as a young one,
aunque ya tuvieramos ochenta.

Let's flow with destiny,
or not,
but let it be.
Without the obstacles imposed by our egos.

You told me
that we, ourselves,
are the makers of our destiny,
so it is time to get ours back
from the hands of uncertainty.

Let's live those dreams that we dream

before they become only words

escapando por la rondijas del tiempo.

Love consists of:
en el amar y en el vivir el amor
like we promised to our wise young selves.

Let's love each other
as we really love ourselves.

I Have to Let You Go

It is me.

I have been walking the world leaving broken pieces of myself,
but just realized how broken my heart really is.
And before I make you pay,
I will let you go...
Only time can make you come back or not...

I have to work on myself.
Review,
step back into my childhood
to unravel the secrets of my own life,
y así *desentrañar* the daddy issues
I did not know I had.

Revisit and knock on each door
of my past traumas.
To not escape,
not even fight them,
but to understand them,
hug them
until these traumas
feel listened to.

As I wish I would have been listened to
when I was a little girl.

So I can be there for myself,
before you.
And then perhaps
later I can learn to be there for you too.

I am not ready yet,
and you are not ready now.

"The lift-off of the doves" by Áurea María.
Pencil and charcoal 8X11, 2024.

Self

Soy yo, Siendo una Paloma

Soy you siendo
una paloma,
fluctuando con el aire.
A mi propio paso.
Empezando a tenerme paciencia,
más compasión,
más respeto a mis sueños
y más transparente con mi misión
de hablar mi voz,
en combinación con mis alas y mi meta.
Aún soy yo siendo una paloma,
cayendo
y sintiéndome en incendio
cuando el destino
o más bien mis miedos
se ponen pesados
y me atacan como parásitos.
Alimentándose de mis propios errores
para debilitarme.
Y me hacen casi estrellarme
en el lodo de la depresión.

Que no me atrape,
porque voy a pelearle,
porque de mis cenizas
necesito levantarme para seguir
en esta cita conmigo misma,
a re-encontrarme.
A liberarme, voy.

Y lograr volar libre
como lo quiero.

Being a Dove

It is me
being dove,
fluctuating in the air
at my own pace.
Starting to be patient with myself
having more compassion,
having more respect for my dreams
and being more transparent with my mission
to speak my voice,
in combination with my wings and my goals.
Nourishing myself from my own errrors to grow.

Still, it's me being a dove
falling down
and feeling on fire
when destiny
or rather my fears
get heavy
and attack me like parasites.
and leech onto my own mistakes
to weaken me.
That almost made me crash
into the mud of depression.

Don't let it catch me,
because I'm going to fight it,
because of my ashes
I need to get up to continue
on this date with myself,
to find myself again.
To free myself, I go.

To manage to fly free
how I want it.

My Fear, My Enemy, And Friend

Fear, *él* takes me from a *sopetón, y me aplasta.*
Overtakes my thoughts,
eyes and *alma.*
Takes away my dreams
from my hands,
me *los arrancha,*
soaking me into
this dark nostalgia.

> *Buddy,*
> *we have been roommates for so long,*
> *that at the end, what do you want me to do?*
> *I am just a simple human,*
> *a brute dummy on how to play the game of life,*
> *an allower of the trespassing of pain,*
> *not a great handler of my own lions.*

You, cruel *amigo,*
you want to heal me
a *fuerza de empujones,*
making me fall
and by dragging me around.

Each day you grow more in me
hungrier,
nosier,
feeding
de un banquete
on my trauma.

With your strange soft hands,
you try to choke me with my weakness,

It, *él* ?
It is the only daily guarantee for me.

Even though I have told you
that I hate the smell of my own vulnerability.

I hate it to death.

Look at him,
There, Fear is in the corner
acurrucándose,
resting.

Me, just laughing
at my own foreign smile.
What else can I do,
but continue to cry?

I think I will miss him if he is gone.
He has been that loyal companion
that I wonder about,

Is he the devil himself
or an angel?
que viene a devorarme
o a salvarme?

Should I stop running from him
or is it better to start hugging him, and
embracing him?

My dear,
my perpetual enemy.
I thought you were my frenemy,
but perhaps you were my only real friend,
who knows all of my secrets from A to Z,
the only one bugging me for attention,
and of course,
the one that hurts me real good
and for my own good,
y sin piedad.

He faces me against myself,
for the crucial battle,
crushing my face,
again and again in the pavement,
con cada mentira,
con cada huída
es peor
esta herida.
The wound never closes.

                                        Hey friend,
                                I am so beaten up
                    that I think I finally understand,
                            If I do not surrender,
                I will get rotten from the inside out
        fulfilling the catastrophe you wish upon me.

I'm going to feel it now or never!
There is only one path left!

            Y tú? Si, tú, amiga? The one that writes.
            Forgiveness?
            Empathy?
            So much for others.
            And for me?
            You do not hold back,
            radically torturing me with *disque* your care.

            How much patience or love is left
            for your most *terca* one, this hard-headed lady?
            The one behind the smoke victim curtain,
            the very same one that holds your lash,
            and now the pencil.
            Have you thought about her?
            Maybe even fear is being a better friend than

Maybe he is trying to protect me
by teaching me with tough love.

Amigo,
Let's start to feel your power
the energy of the feeling fearless intruding,
letting go lo guardado,
finally counter-producing
what fear is supposed to make in us.

Letting ourselves heal with our own hurts,
our own fears.
Living the process to its max,
as it should have been since the very beginning.

We are just humans,
and we have to fall to learn.
It is the cruel truth.
And what is a life
without living the battle
and surviving
and coming out taming
esos monstruosos dragones?

Live the process and
saborea el miedo

See, how the flavor has changed.
Try! It is the only way.

That cold feeling
has now become a warm one.
Now, it is not only fear...
It is healing.

Personal

When the abuse becomes
what am I,
"The selfish one who steals your time,
the one that invades you and crosses your path,
the one who demands without reason,
the one who stresses you with her stupidities."

When you convince me of what you think of me.
When my freedom smells only like stinking selfishness to you.
And I end up *comiéndome la historia,*
without almost no hesitation,
and I don't have a fix anymore.

At that moment,
she comes to me,
that girl,
to whom no one would tell her what to think,
if she did not believe it...

The same one
that looked at the truth without a doubt,
sure and with a strong step.

The one
who was not going to take it from her uncle
who did not treat her father's sister well.

The same girl
who counted on herself,
on "her vast life experience."
She was like a wave,
with intrinsic and natural force.

She is telling me now,

> *Don't take it personally!*
> *It is his own wound,*
> *from where he speaks to you*
> *of the miseries he feels about himself*
> *don't you see?*

But *niña*, it feels personal,
and it hurts,
like dry ice bursting
its burning inside my wound,

Maybe you're being insensitive to my pain.

Maybe yes,
I'm just a girl,
but until then,
until you will let it hurt you
you will understand
So, what should you do or not do?
Only hurt?
Keep hurting yourself, perhaps?

Girl, where do you get all this wisdom from,
siendo tan pequeña?

Of the clear eyes that I still have.

With time I don't know
if I will be able to see like I do now,
but I'll try to remind you,
that we share this path.

And I will look for you so that
I can hold your hand.
and tell you,
You are never alone.

Dear Poem Of Healing

Why did you not tell me that healing is more about the process and
that I would be hurt again?
Why did you not tell me that I had to travel back and forth through my
fears?
Why did you not tell me that I had to learn to savor my failures
combined with broken glass and my own blood?

That I will wish I started earlier this *agridulce* journey.
That pain will eventually bring joy.

That I was hidden for too long.
That I was so afraid of living.
That I was going to regret that later.

That I could be move capable of making my demons friends rather
than trying to escape from them.

That those demons could become loyal mates,
and only those who win
are those who learn to play with death
and survive,
but still can live fully,

completa.

"The transformation of the Butterfly" by Áurea María.
Photograph of sculpture made of fabric and wood elements,
4 feet x 1 feet x 1 feet, 2014.

Empowerment

Coming Back After The Gray World

Returning to the practical world
after disassembling my soul
in the private of the dark grayness
is gut wrenching scary,
but it is only a temporary trauma.

Every time that eternity of adjusting
is less
demolishing,
weighty,
crashing.
I can understand myself better
every time.

On every trip I bring a new learning experience,
a tool that comes all bloody
because I have taken it away
from the hands of my demons,

a la fuerza también,
tampoco ellos saben como dejar ir.

Even though I have nightmares
of repeating the process
each time the pain is less rough with me
and I slowly become more joyful.

I am more resilient.
I am becoming
just like the person
I dreamed of being.
This is who I want to be,
me.

I Was Born Alone

I know I was born alone,
saying it to myself
is a double punch in my reality,
here in my chest,
in the guts *de mi corazón*
and the memories of past and present.

"You were born alone."
So easy to say by others,
When leaving a relationship behind,
it is hurtful sarcasm.

"You were born alone!"
Laughing at my crying face inside.
My cries hidden
so others won't see.
I, to maintain my dignity
force a smile.

It has been a difficult road
with so many bumps,
quebradas,
and ditches,
I have fallen so many times.

Life has played a trick on me,
implanting hesitations,
just to make me lose
the strength I have gained.

"You were born alone."
It is going to only hurt me
until I learn to read as it is,
a phrase.

Read it just as it is,
Singleton,
the delivery of a unique human being.

Read it as a child does,

free of the pain
I sometimes place on things.

Read it with joy,
like it should be read.

Then,
say it louder.
Louder!
Because it is true.

I was born alone.
I am blessed twice.
I am reborn.
I can live life alone.

All the strength I need
is just in me.
I just need to explore it
and explode it.

I can live alone
and live life with all its colors,
the way I decide it.

The Mess Of the House

Now, the Mess talks to me.
He tells me that he is happy now.
He no longer brings
his friend Depression with him.
It's just him, a quiet Mess.

It is no longer accompanied by Guilt,
so insistent and overwhelming.

This Mess is now only mine,
and he tells me
that he isn't bothered
to be by my side anymore,
He says that I have learned to live with him.
That I no longer hate him to the point of despair.
Guilt, his usual friend has lost his power over me,
and is resting at least for now.

Igual, ya saben y you sé
quién es la dueña de la casa,

YO,
Yo soy quién manda.

Sing and cry

Shout your music and your heart out,
crying your eyes out more than ever,
or sing it to yourself.
Only just mumble it like a murmur of the sea,
Musítala como tú quieras.

To liberate the last of your demons
or to caress your scars.
Como tú quieras.

Let that tear, that was contained, to flow
because pain no longer limits you.
You already surpassed .
Take the consciousness
that the pain is transforming in your strength
and rooted it in your soul.

Scream in your singing,
angrily,
dishearteningly,
tearfully,
blinded from confusion,

*desmenuzando tus heridas
remachándolas,*
repairing the tissues of your voice,
seeing inside yourself,
hopeful.

Sob if you need to,
but sing.
Continue and continue
against your own fear
of failing to not get to the other side
of your own dark moments.
You are about to get there...
Hold on to what you have,
and who you are.

Sing it out,
all out...

Your voice is reborn.

It is yours.
Take it.

Hazla tuya
porque es sólo tuya,
Única.

Sprouting My Strength My Wings

My wound has sprouted
my vulnerable strength,
I didn't know I had some strength left,
nor could I use it to empower myself.

Even through,
the pain of peeling the skin
of my own fears
has been torture,
having a naked soul of self-doubt,
feels liberating.

Within the protection of my chrysalis,
it has enabled me to internally grow.

Nurturing my soul,
and maturing my wings.
I had finally achieved my metamorphosis
I am the butterfly I want to be.

I am proud of myself.

Por fin,
soy la mariposa de fuego
que mi niña interior
quiso para nosotras.

Estoy aprendiendo a volar de nuevo.

Ahora comienzo una nueva historia.

She Is Coming Out to Shout Her Truth

Finally my voice comes out
in a scream
my foremost truth.
The one that is me.
The bad dye that stained me
from my past and affected my future
has already dissolved
because I can finally articulate words.

Mi voz,
she was stuck between
your merciless darts,
and your silent treatment.

She was restrained,
amordazada
by blame and outrage,
kidnappers of self-esteem.

To guard the minimal
peace in the home
it just highlighted
her emotional limitations more.

She was fading.
She was drowning.
She was facing death
She was almost succumbing

She had to confront,
She had to fight and fight and fight.
She thought she had died,
But she survived.

Her voice came out all scratchy,
rasposa, desmoronada
and
I was afraid to push her,
speak for her,
I was afraid to break her,

De rematarla.
She looked really weak,
but she became stronger.

De tanto coraje guardado.

The tiredness of being silent for so long,
made her question herself at first,

but

It gave her a boost like a kick-start,
There was no further ground to fall on,
There was no longer any place to get stuck
She could no longer be trapped.

Your noise will no longer turn off my channel,
my throat,
my sound,
my song,
my voice.

She has been reborn!

She is here to speak her truth!

Discovering me

I finally fell in love
with me,
observing from close and
appreciating the roots of my self-doubts
that rain down
on the panorama of my life,
in my moments of confusion,
tinted in gray.
But who knew it would be so many shades of gray.

To reassemble my memories and rewrite my destiny.

It's not just decoration to the gloomy landscape
They are flashes of my mind
alerting me that something still remains to be discovered.

It was exhausting to keep trying to understand
my confused self,
in the midst of
mis tormentas personales
and your unpredictable moods.
At this point in life,
when I should have known every inch of me already.

But it I am ok now.
I have practiced
through all kinds of weather,
through all kinds of seas.
Ya le agarré la onda.
Now, it has actually become my favorite sport.

Ando, decifrándome, descubriéndome todavía.
There is no rush
I am starting to indulge in myself.
I like who I am now
despite the fear or pain.

Ando,
esculcándome,
pero perdonándome también.

Slowing down,
to enjoy the ride
to live my life in the present, not as before.
Learning to cultivate kindness to myself.

Ando, *cuidándome con cariño,*
holding my own hand
and listening to my own cries
with patience.

Letting go,
so I can feel the light
and bathe in it and receive all its power,
empowering my heart with it.

I have discovered my own way to heal
and my true values.
Life makes sense again.

To find all the levels of my consciousness,
so they can be one.

She Is Back

The one you missed is back
after shedding her old skin.

Y consegui una nueva piel.
Ya esta lista para salir de el cocoon.

That energy you loved is taking root again,
but I don't want others to know it, yet.

She needs to be built solid
so she will be almost unbreakable
for future battles.

So she could fly in the fire
and not get burnt, but absorb it
and morph with it,

volviéndose una mariposa de fuego.
Salvándose a sí misma,
una héroe de su propia vida.

Nothing will scare her again.
She has been facing
every one of her demons.

She has fought so much
that she has torn off every scab
just to heal it.
This time it is real.

She is here to stay.

Me

Aurea,
Áurea,
I haven't used the accent mark in my name ever until now.
I still struggle to capitalize it and put the accent mark on it.

Not recognizing my name as it should
has become the antithesis of my childhood superpowers,

Not recognizing its grammar rules and sound
in its greatness openly,
it was betrayal
to my own values
Blasphemy!

Not recognizing its meaning
as more than one
and as something precious as gold itself
and the beauty of a flower
is one more sacrilege.

I have been blind and deaf to my real person.

Not recognizing my name,
is not recognizing my own self.

Not recognizing the figure in the mirror.

Es sepulatarme viva.
Y es que no puedo verme acaso?

Fog that doesn't move from the view,
una neblina que no se disipa,
between my name and me
has existed for too long.

I have inherited,

and carried the family name

y ellas también,

starting from my great grandmother,
my grandmother,
my mother,
and myself.

Inferiority complex,
sabotage,

falta de amor propio,
desarraigo.

But from what I have seen
I have learned.
The *subconscious lineage* of pain stops here
with me.

I am the last *Amazona.*
I am the vindicator
of my lineage
I represent the women in my family,
and I am creating a
new woman lineage,

As a mother,
as a daughter,
as myself,
Áurea.

"My own Phoenix o transformation/
Mi propio Fénix o Transformación" by Áurea María.
Acrylic, 15 x20 inches framed, 2016.

About the Author

Áurea María Altamirano Cuaresma was born in Lima, Peru. She studied Language and Literature, and graduated with a B.A. in Child Development from *Federico Villarreal National University* from Peru. Soon later, she worked as a preschool teacher, and migrated to Berkeley, Ca. in 2008, to work as *au pair* and continue her studies. She currently works at BAHIA, a bilingual afterschool program in Berkeley. She also teaches Spanish at *Centro Latino Language School*, to individuals, and in groups around the Bay Area and in Berkeley, California.

Back in her home country, Peru, she was a member, writer, and collaborator of two student literary magazines at her university, *Ática y Katarsis* in 2001 and 2002.

She also is a participant at Community Literature Initiative (CLI), an organization dedicated to supporting minority writers. She published some of her poems in the newspaper *Berkeley Times*, in its *Annual Poetry Edition*, in 2018, 2019, 2021, 2022 and 2023. She has published some of her paintings, drawings, and photography in *Milvia Street Journal*, a journal of Berkeley City college, in 2016, 2017, 2018 and 2019.

She also was invited to be a judge for school-aged children's writing essays and poems at *In Dulci Jubilo*, an Annual Children Writing Contest, for the Elementary Schools in Berkeley, in 2017, 2018 and 2019.

She also was an Altar maker at "The Day of the Dead Oakland Festival" in 2016, 2017, 2018, 2019 and 2021 sponsored by *The Unity Council* and the city of Oakland, in California. She also build altars at the Berkeley Day of the Dead Festival in Berkeley, in 2021. She had some group bilingual exhibitions: *Perú, It's History and*

People in 2018 and 2017, and a solo-bilingual exhibition dedicated to Latina Mother's day, *Mother's day*, at Centro Latino Language School in Berkeley, in 2019, and another art show, called *Women* at El Comal Gallery, in Vallejo, in 2016.

She participated in the painting and design of the mural, *From Incarceration to Liberation*, and with some art pieces related to the mural creation in its subsequent Exhibitions and Receptions Shows, in 2015 and 2018 at the San Francisco State University in collaboration with *The True Colors Mural Project Group*.

She participated at *The Student Art Show*, at the Jerry Adams Gallery of Berkeley City College, in 2015 and 2016. Later, she joined *The Latin American Club* at Berkeley City College in 2015, with their support she created GALA, *The Club de Artes Latinoamericanas* at Berkeley City College, to create a space for the Latino voices in writing bilingual poetry and to show their art work. Later, she organized and performed at *The Poetry at the Altar and Open Mic Event*, sponsored by GALA Club, 2016 in Berkeley and also organized the group art exhibit, *Las artes Latinoamericanas*, in 2017 and the event *The Latino Art Show*, 2018.

Conect with Áurea: She is always willing to take on new students to teach them Spanish.
Website: Aureamaria.com
       Instagram: Aurea484
       Facebook: AureaMaria Altamirano

Áurea is a teacher at heart, mom, daughter, a writer, a visual artist and eternal student of life.

Publishers Note

Daxson publishing was created to help marginalized artists publish their work, so the world can hear their voice. The vision for this publishing house is to help people get their work out there, and not have them struggle finding their way through the publishing process. Everyone's voice deserves to be heard, and we are here to help. If you are interested in submitting a manuscript, email daxsonpublishing@gmail.com.

www.ingramcontent.com/pod-product-compliance
Lightning Source LLC
Chambersburg PA
CBHW051315120626

46547CB00015B/2247